BR STEAM IN ACTION

ROGER SIVITER ARPS
GREAT BEAR PUBLISHING

The down "Bournemouth Belle", 12.30 ex Waterloo, is seen on 10 September 1966 near Brockenhurst, on the edge of the New Forest, hauled by ex SR Merchant Navy Class Pacific No 35012 *United States Lines*. The "Belle" was always locomotive hauled until its final run on Sunday 9 July 1967. By this time, many of the ex SR Pacifics had lost their nameplates and crests, however, as can be seen, this was not the case with No 35012. (*Ken Hale*)

A scene from the very last day of BR steam - 11 August 1968. "Black Five" 4-6-0 No 45110 pauses at Rainhill with the Liverpool to Manchester section of the "15 Guinea Special". The crowds are gathering for one "last look" at steam, and within minutes there were hundreds of people in this area. Notice the number of children present in their Dads' arms and on their shoulders.

(*Roger Siviter*)

Introduction

This book is to commemorate the 40th anniversary of the end of steam traction on British Railways (BR). The bulk of the book (90 pages) is an overview of steam at work between 1964 and the end of steam on 11 August 1968 – the famous "15 Guinea Special". This is followed by a short section (6 pages) showing main line steam activity post-1968.

In compiling this book, I am very grateful to Hugh Ballantyne and Ken Hale for use of their splendid pictures: to my wife Christina for much help: and last but not least to the BR staff who make it all possible

Roger Siviter, ARPS.
Teignmouth, Devon, 2008

© Roger Siviter 2008
Published by Great Bear Publishing
2 Seacliff, First Drive, Dawlish Road, Teignmouth, Devon TQ14 8TX
 Tel: 01626 774787

£19.99

ISBN 978-095411508-1

Designed and printed by Ian Allan Ltd, Hersham, Surrey KT12 4RG

Front Cover:
On 17 July 1965, ex LNER Class B1 4-6-0 No 61180 climbs through the rock cutting at North Queensferry before crossing the Forth Bridge with an up troop train. *(Ken Hale)*

Below: Ex GWR Class 1400 0-4-2T No 1453 and auto coach No W244W pull away from Sharpness with the 16.15 to Berkeley Road on 26 September 1964. These Collett designed locomotives were first introduced in 1932 for light branch work, and were push-and-pull fitted. *(Hugh Ballantyne)*

4

Top Left: Veteran North British Class J37 0-6-0 No 64585 takes the Edinburgh line at Hilton junction with a short freight train on 27 March 1964. These pre-grouping locomotives were first introduced in 1914 and designed by W. P. Reid.

(Ken Hale)

Bottom Left: On 17 July 1965, ex LNER Class B1 4-6-0 No 61180 climbs through the rock cutting at North Queensferry before crossing the Forth Bridge with an up troop train.

(Ken Hale)

Above: The unique ex LNER Class V2 2-6-2 No 60813 (being the only member of the Class fitted with smoke deflectors) hurries along near Aberdour with the 09.10 (Saturday only) Dundee to Blackpool train. No 60813 was shedded at Dundee, which over the years was famous for its fine fleet of Class V2 2-6-2s. 20 August 1966.

(Ken Hale)

Left, Bottom and Top Right: These next three pictures were taken on 21 September 1966 and the location is Copmanthorpe, a few miles south of York on the main route to Leeds. They also show the variety of locomotives still to be seen in this area in 1966.

The first picture shows Class V2 2-6-2 No 60831 and brake van as it heads south on the morning of that day. Later in the afternoon we see Standard Class 9F No 92016 with a lengthy southbound goods. And the final picture at Copmanthorpe shows ex LMS Jubilee Class 4-6-0 No 45593 *Kholapur* (now happily preserved) with a mixed southbound goods - a somewhat lowly task for an express passenger engine.

(Three pictures: Roger Siviter)

Bottom Right: We complete this quartet of north-eastern scenes with ex LNER Class K1 2-6-0 No 62060 (and brake van) as it heads south through Church Fenton on the York to Leeds line, and junction station for the line to Castleford, on 26 May 1966.

(Roger Siviter)

A fine picture of ex LNER Gresley A4 Pacific No 60024 *Kingfisher* as it heads north near Inverkeithing with a Millerhill to Aberdeen freight, on 17 July 1965. The locomotive was working back to its home shed of Ferryhill (Aberdeen) having previously worked the Saturdays Only 09.10 Aberdeen to Edinburgh passenger train.

(Ken Hale)

Left: With a wonderful display of exhaust, ex LMS Stanier Class 8F 2-8-0 No 48090 climbs the 1 in 132 at Little Salkeld (on the Settle to Carlisle route) with a south bound goods train. The date of this lovely autumn day is 4 November 1967. *(Ken Hale)*

Above: Earlier in 1967 (6 May) and still on the former Midland Railway S & C route we see Class 9F 2-10-0 No 92071 as it approaches Ais Gill summit with a south bound goods. The gradient here is 1 in 100. Dominating the background is Wild Boar Fell. *(Ken Hale)*

Above:
On Good Friday 1966 (8 April) an immaculate Bullied Merchant Navy Class Pacific No 35022 *Holland - America Line* speeds along the old LSWR four-track main line near Basing with a morning Waterloo to Bournemouth train. Already there are signs of electrification work, which would be complete by July of the following year.

(Roger Siviter)

Top Right:
A busy scene at Salisbury station on 24 August 1964. West Country Class Pacific No 34095 *Brentor* is rolling to a halt with the "Atlantic Coast Express" ("ACE") which departed from Waterloo at 11.00, final destination being Plymouth, with various portions for North Devon and North Cornwall. On the right hand side in the bay platform is Standard Class 5MT 4-6-0 No 73119 waiting to follow the "ACE" down the West of England line with the 12.36 all-stations to Exeter. Note the LSWR lamp fittings and semaphore signals.

(Hugh Ballantyne)

Bottom Right:
On 27 March 1965, West Country Pacific No 34037 *Clovelly* heads down the bank at Parkstone (west of Bournemouth) with a Waterloo to Weymouth train.

(Ken Hale)

Ex GWR Castle Class 4-6-0 No 7023 *Penrice Castle* departs from Bath Green Park station on 7 June 1964 and heads north to Gloucester and then to Paddington with a Home Counties Railway Society special train. This train started from Waterloo at 08.54, with a two hour run to Bournemouth behind a Merchant Navy Class Pacific. At Bournemouth, an S & D 2-8-0 No 53807 and Class 4F 0-6-0 No 44558 took over for the journey over the Somerset and Dorset line to Bath Green Park. This was the first time that a Castle Class locomotive had visited Green Park station.

(Hugh Ballantyne)

BR Standard Class 5MT 4-6-0 No 73073 leaves the Manchester line and sweeps past Winwick junction box on the West Coast Main Line (WCML) with the 10.31 Manchester to Bangor train. Behind the train can be seen ex LMS Class 5MT 4-6-0 No 44958 held at signals on the WCML with the 09.51 (Saturdays Only) Blackpool to London Euston train. 28 August 1965. (*Hugh Ballantyne*)

Above & Below: Still on the WCML, this time at Shap Incline in Cumberland. Ex LMS Class 8F 2-8-0 No 48200 approaches Scout Green signal box on the afternoon of 29 March 1966 with a heavy north bound mixed goods train, and is given a helping hand in the shape of ex LMS Fairburn Class 4MT 2-6-4T No 42154, one of the regular banking engines shedded at Tebay (12E).

(*Two pictures: Roger Siviter*)

Top Right: This next picture, taken on Shap on the same day as the previous pictures only a few minutes later, shows "Black Five" 4-6-0 No 44779 climbing the 1 in 75 near Scout Green box with the 13.25 Crewe to Carlisle goods train.

(*Roger Siviter*)

Bottom Right: The final picture in this Shap quartet shows Class 5MT 4-6-0 No 45420, having climbed Shap bank, running downhill towards Shap station with a Crewe to Carlisle van train. The road in the background is the A6. This picture was also taken on 29 March 1966.

(*Roger Siviter*)

Above: BR Standard Class 9F 2-10-0 No 92077 heads south through Church Fenton on 26 May 1966. The semaphore signals are LNER and the signal box just visible behind the water column is of NER origin. This class of heavy freight locomotives was first introduced in 1954 and worked almost until the end of steam, No 92077 being one of the last to remain in service. It was withdrawn from Carnforth shed in June 1968.

(Roger Siviter)

Right: This early LNER wooden posted gallows type signal dominates the scene as Class 5MT 4-6-0 No 44858 takes water at Nottingham Victoria station (ex GCR) on Thursday 1 September 1966, before leaving with the 17.15 train to London Marylebone. The following weekend (3 September) would see the end of the through workings on the old GCR route between Nottingham Victoria and London Marylebone.

(Roger Siviter)

Top & Bottom: As late as 1967, pre-grouping North Eastern Railway locomotives were to be found at work in the North East. On 22 September 1965, Class J27 0-6-0 No 65853 is seen at Ryhope Grange junction with coal empties from Sunderland Docks. These locomotives were first introduced in 1906, and designed by W. Worsdell.

The second scene shows Class Q6 0-8-0 No 63455 in the sidings at Pelaw with a coal train waiting to go up to Consett. These powerful freight locomotives were designed for the NER by Sir Vincent Raven and introduced in 1913. 20 September 1965.

(Two pictures: Hugh Ballantyne)

Top: This third North Eastern picture was taken at South Pelaw on 20 September 1965, only this time not with a pre-grouping locomotive but with one of the BR Standard Class 9F 2-10-0s, No 92060. The locomotive has just passed South Pelaw signal box with a load of iron ore bound for the steel works at Consett.

(Hugh Ballantyne)

Bottom: The Cromford & High Peak Railway in Derbyshire would close by the end of April 1967, however in 1966 there was still a certain amount of activity on this mineral line. On 20 May 1966, Class 0F 0-4-0ST No 47000 shunts wagons at Middleton Quarry. The first five members of this class of outside cylindered 0-4-0STs were first introduced in 1932, and designed by Kitson to Stanier's requirements for the LMS. The last five members of the class (Nos 47005 - 9) were introduced in 1953 with extended side tanks and coal space.

(Roger Siviter)

Top Left: On 12 March 1966, Class 8F 2-8-0 No 48665, banked by ex GWR Class 5600 0-6-2T No 5605, climbs towards Brymbo Steel Works with an iron ore train from Croes Newydd yard - Wrexham.
(Ken Hale)

Bottom Left: Shunting in Brymbo Steel Works exchange sidings / yard on 7 May 1966 is Class 8F 2-8-0 No 48747 from Croes Newydd. Alongside the 2-8-0 is one of the steelworks' fleet of Yorkshire Engine Co. diesel locomotives. *(Roger Siviter)*

Above: Leaving Ellesmere Port on 10 December 1966 with an east bound freight train is one of the few remaining members of the Hughes / Fowler Class 5MT 2-6-0s, No 42859. These locomotives were popularly known as "Crabs". *(Ken Hale)*

On a warm summer's day in 1967 (17 July) BR Standard Class 7P6F Britannia Pacific No 70013 (formerly *Oliver Cromwell*) effortlessly climbs the 1 in 100 up to Ais Gill summit with the 13.10 Carlisle to Skipton goods train. The train is just passing over Ais Gill viaduct, a mile north of Ais Gill summit. This locomotive was the only active member of the class in 1968, and was the motive power for the Manchester to Carlisle section of the "15 Guinea Special" on 11 August of that year. It was then preserved at Bressingham Gardens in Norfolk. It is now being put into working order at the Great Central Railway at Loughborough, and is scheduled to work special charters in this 40th commemorative year, and hopefully it will be used on the repeat of the "15 Guinea Special" on 10 August.

(*Ken Hale*)

Top Left: Saturday 20 August 1966 on the Cambrian line around the Talerddig area proved to be a lovely sunny day, and amongst the many pictures that were taken that day - for there were several photographers (and recordists) in action - was this one, of BR Standard Class 4MT 4-6-0 No 75002, seen here near Talerddig station with an afternoon Machynlleth to Shrewsbury stopping train.

(*Roger Siviter*)

Bottom Left: Seen on the four track section between Llandudno Junction and Colwyn Bay is BR Standard Class 5MT 4-6-0 No 73157 with a morning Bangor to Manchester train. 6 September 1966.

(*Roger Siviter*)

Above: The final picture in this trio of Welsh pictures was taken at 5.40 p.m. on 5 September 1966, and shows "Black Five" 4-6-0 No 45279 as it runs through Conway with an up mixed goods train.

(*Roger Siviter*)

Above: Our next location is Garsdale water troughs, the highest in the country. These were situated just south of Garsdale station on the Settle to Carlisle route. On 12 August 1967, Class 5 MT No 44943 speeds over the troughs with a south bound goods train. The shed plate 55A indicates that this is a Leeds Holbeck engine.

(*Ken Hale*)

Right: We are still on the S & C route, this time just north of Newbiggin, some five miles north of the market town of Appleby. Ex LMS Ivatt Class 4MT 2-6-0 No 43049 (shedded at Carlisle Kingmoor 12A) is framed by this famous stone built farm occupation bridge as it heads south with a trip working from Carlisle to Appleby, on 19 July 1967.

(*Ken Hale*)

Top: Ex SR U Class 2-6-0 No 31809 is just about to depart from Reading's Southern station with the 09.45 to Redhill on 24 October 1964. Steam haulage on this route would finish in a few weeks' time, on 3 January 1965. Worthy of note are the platform canopies and support columns. *(Hugh Ballantyne)*

Bottom: Exeter St Davids station is our next location as unrebuilt Battle of Britain Class Pacific No 34054 *Lord Beaverbrook* waits to leave this west country station with the 10.15 (Sundays) to Ilfracombe on 3 May 1964. Note the milk wagons - return empties. *(Hugh Ballantyne)*

Top Right: Veteran Class O2 0-4-4T No 24 *Calbourne* waits to leave Brading on the Isle of Wight with the 13.10 Ryde to Shanklin train.

The date is 21 July 1966. These former LSWR locomotives were first introduced in 1889, and designed by W. Adams. The semaphore signals are of SR rail built design. *(Roger Siviter)*

Bottom Right: The scene at Penzance station on 3 May 1964, with West Country Pacific No 34002 *Salisbury* having just arrived with a steam special from Exeter, organised by the RCTS. The first section from Exeter to Plymouth (and return) was in the hands of ex GWR Class 2800 2-8-0 No 2887, with No 34002 in charge from Plymouth to Penzance and return. This train was named the "Cornubian". This would be the last steam to visit Penzance for some 34 years, until the visit of ex GWR King Class 4-6-0 No 6024 *King Edward I* on 19 September 1998. *(Hugh Ballantyne)*

Ex LMS Jubilee Class 4-6-0 No 45593 *Kholapur* climbs up to Horton in Ribblesdale on 29 July 1967 with a St Pancras to Glasgow train.

The location is Batty Wood, where the S & C line crosses over the River Ribble.

(Ken Hale)

Above: On 14 May 1965, BR Standard Class 9F 2-10-0 No 92206 passes by Undy water troughs, situated between Magor and Severn Tunnel Junction with an up empty mineral train. *(Hugh Ballantyne)*

Below: BR Standard Class 4MT 2-6-0 No 76013 leaves Bath Green Park station with the 13.10 local train to Templecombe. 6 March 1965. *(Hugh Ballantyne)*

Top: The RCTS Scot Commemorative tour from Crewe to Carlisle, outward via the S & C route and return on the WCML, is seen pausing at Blackburn station where ex LMS Royal Scot 4-6-0 No 46115 *Scots Guardsman* took water. The date is 13 February 1965. (See also picture on page 43).   (*Hugh Ballantyne*)

Bottom: A very pleasant scene at Cosford on the evening of 24 August 1964, as ex LMS Jubilee Class 4-6-0 No 45577 *Bengal*, shedded at Shrewsbury, then 6D, waits to leave the station with the 17.38 Wolverhampton to Shrewsbury train. Note the wooden station platforms and buildings. This station is situated by the RAF base, which can be seen through the gap in the station buildings on the left hand side.   (*Ken Hale*)

Top: Ex LMS Class 7F 0-8-0 No 48895 pauses during shunting duties at the ex Midland Railway goods depot at Wednesfield Road, Wolverhampton. 4 May 1964. (See also picture on page 42). (*Ken Hale*)

Bottom: A splendid sight at Swindon shed on 9 May 1964 as one of Stanier's ex LMS Coronation Class Pacifics, No 46251 *City of Nottingham*, stands outside the former GWR shed before returning to Nottingham with the RCTS special "The East Midlander No 7 Rail Tour". On the left can be seen the front end of ex GWR Castle Class 4-6-0 No 7022 *Hereford Castle*. (*Hugh Ballantyne*)

Top: Former GWR Class 5700 0-6-0PTs Nos 9615 and 9656 pose outside Radyr shed (Glamorgan) on the 13 May 1965.

(*Hugh Ballantyne*)

Bottom: Last Spring for the "Chalford Flyer" as ex GWR Class 1400 0-4-2T No 1451 takes water at Stroud on 26 March 1964 whilst working the 13.03 Gloucester to Chalford service.

(*Hugh Ballantyne*)

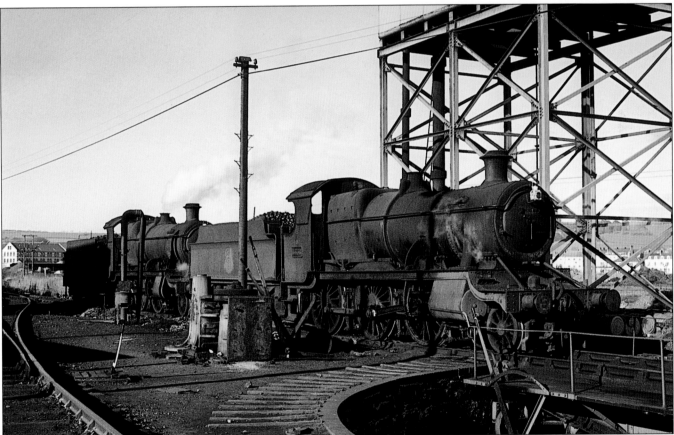

Top: Hall Class 4-6-0 No 7915 *Mere Hall* looks in smart external condition as it prepares to leave Birmingham Snow Hill station on the evening of 25 August 1964 with the 17.45 train to Evesham via Stourbridge Junction and Worcester Shrub Hill station. By the following year, almost without exception, ex GWR locomotives would lose their brass cabside plates and, where applicable, their attractive nameplates. *(Ken Hale)*

Bottom: Another 1964 GWR scene, this time at Barnstaple shed on 29 February 1964. Standing in the shed yard by the turntable are two ex GWR Class 4300 2-6-0s Nos 5336 and 6345. For many years these locomotives were the mainstay of the Taunton to Barnstaple service. *(Hugh Ballantyne)*

Top: On 16 May 1964, ex LNER A4 Pacific No 60016 *Silver King* approaches Gleneagles station with the up Postal train, 15.30 ex Aberdeen. No 60016 moved to Scotland from Gateshead in late 1963, but was withdrawn from service in March 1965. On the left of the picture is the line to Crieff. Note also the semaphore signals of Caledonian Railway (CR) design. *(Ken Hale)*

Bottom: Ex LNER Class A3 Pacific No 60052 *Prince Palatine* pauses at Galashields on the Waverley route with the 09.50 Edinburgh to Leeds train on 25 July 1964. *(Ken Hale)*

Top: Class B1 4-6-0 No 61134 and "Black Five" 4-6-0 No 45477 burst out of Edinburgh Princes Street station on the 29 August 1964 with the 14.05 train to Manchester and Liverpool. Sadly this station closed completely on 6 September 1965.   (*Ken Hale*)

Bottom: In early 1966, Scottish-based A4 Pacific No 60024 *Kingfisher* visited the south of England and hauled a series of enthusiasts' specials. On 26 March 1966, No 60024 is seen approaching Yeovil Pen Mill station with the "Gresley Society" special from Waterloo to Weymouth and Yeovil, and return to Waterloo. The train has just passed under the SR main line near Yeovil Junction on the run into Pen Mill station.   (*Hugh Ballantyne*)

Top: The "Sussex Downsman" pauses at Partridge Green station (on the Steyning line) on Sunday 22 March 1964 before leaving for Hove and Three Bridges behind ex SR Class N 2-6-0 No 31411. This train was jointly organised by the RCTS and LCGB societies, and aimed to travel by steam power (mainly for the last time) over a number of lines in Sussex, several of which were threatened with the loss of their passenger services. The departure was from Waterloo at 09.00 with a return to London Victoria, using a variety of steam locomotives. *(Hugh Ballantyne)*

Bottom: Another special charter train, this time the LCGB "East Devon Rail Tour" from Waterloo to East Devon. Hauled by ex SR Merchant Navy Pacific No 35022 *Holland - America Line*, the special was photographed nearing Axminster on the outward journey on 7 March 1965. This was the second special train to East Devon organised by the LCGB, the first being on 28 February 1965. *(Hugh Ballantyne)*

Pulling a very mixed freight train, ex LMS Class 5MT 4-6-0 No 44661 approaches the former GWR Snow Hill station from the Hockley direction on 12 August 1966. The climb up Hockley bank is 1 in 47, and although it is only short in distance, trains would often be held awaiting platform space, especially on summer Saturdays. I well remember in my "train spotting" days, from 1948 to 1952, seeing two up trains in Snow Hill's platform 7, and two more waiting to come up from Hockley. Glorious days!

(Roger Siviter)

Top: Ex LMS Class 7F 0-8-0 No 48895 shunts at Wednesfield Road goods depot, Wolverhampton, on 4 May 1964. This splendid looking locomotive was built around 1936 to a much earlier design (1912) by Bowen-Cooke for the LNWR. The last members of this class, which were withdrawn in 1964, were shedded at Bescot (2F) and Bushbury (2K). Note also the LMS on the tender. This former goods depot is now the site of the new Post Office complex.

(*Ken Hale*)

Above: The last ex LMS Royal Scot Class 4-6-0 in service was No 46115 *Scots Guardsman*, seen here on 13 February 1965 on the RCTS "Rebuilt Scot Commemorative Tour" as it draws its stock forward at Carlisle to place at platform for the return journey to Crewe via the WCML, the outward journey from Crewe to Carlisle having been via the S & C route.

(*Hugh Ballantyne*)

43

Top Left, Bottom Left , Right and Below: By 1966, with one or two exceptions, the ex WD Class 8F 2-8-0s were mainly to be found operating between Hull and Goole and the Wakefield areas of Yorkshire, as these next four pictures show.

The first scene shows No 90699 shunting at Castleford goods depot before leaving with a west bound van train. 26 May 1966.

In our second picture, also taken on 26 May 1966, we see No 90210 as it heads northwards past Wakefield shed (56A) with a coal train from the Goole area.

The next picture shows No 90112 heading out of Wakefield on the line to Goole with a mixed goods train. 13 July 1966.

Our final picture was taken on 20 September 1966, and shows No 90339 leaving Wakefield and heading for Goole with a train of empty coal wagons.

(*Four pictures: Roger Siviter*)

Top: On 16 April 1965, one of Sir Nigel Gresley's A4 Pacifics No 60009 *Union of South Africa* pulls out of Stirling station with the 17.30 Glasgow to Aberdeen train. No 60009, along with several other members of this famous class of locomotive, has been preserved, and over the years many of them have been seen on main line special trains.

(*Ken Hale*)

Above: The only member of the ex LNER A2 Pacific Class to be preserved is No 60532 *Blue Peter*, seen here in its BR days as it approaches North Queensferry and the Forth Bridge with an up freight train, on 17 July 1965. This locomotive, like some members of the A4 Class Pacifics, has been seen main line charter work.

(*Ken Hale*)

Above & Right: Right until the end of steam in their areas, the three principal banks on the WCML north of Crewe - Grayrigg, Shap and Beattock - all used steam traction to bank heavy trains up these steep gradients. These next two pictures show the "bankers" at work on Shap and Beattock (the Grayrigg banker is on page 75).

The first view, taken from the level crossing by Scout Green signal box, Shap, on 25 June 1966 shows ex LMS Class 4MT 2-6-4T No 42251 banking a heavy north bound goods, which is hauled by Britannia Pacific No 70040 *Clive of India.*

The second picture, taken just north of Beattock station on 24 June 1966, shows BR Standard Class 4MT 2-6-0 No 76098 banking a north bound van train, hauled by Class 5MT 4-6-0 No 45125.

(*Two pictures: Roger Siviter*)

Left: In the late spring of 1964, Class 9F 2-10-0 No 92139 (shedded at Saltley, 21A) tops the famous Lickey Bank and runs through Blackwell station with a north bound freight train.
(Roger Siviter collection)

Top Right: This was the scene at Bath Green Park station on the last day of public operation - 5 March 1966. An Ivatt Class 2MT 2-6-2 is waiting to leave with a local train. *(Ken Hale)*

Bottom Right: Another Ivatt Class 2MT 2-6-2, this time No 41212, arrives at the attractive station at Stamford (Lincolnshire) with the 09.35 push-and-pull train from Seaton on 16 September 1965. This unique service finished by the end of 1965. *(Hugh Ballantyne)*

Below: A work-stained and weary ex GWR Class 43XX 2-6-0 No 5336, at this time the oldest surviving member of its class (built at Swindon in 1917), stands at Dulverton station waiting to leave with the 13.15 Taunton to Barnstaple train on 29 February 1964. This line closed on 3 October 1966.
(Hugh Ballantyne)

Stanier three-cylinder Jubilee Class 4-6-0 No 45565 *Victoria* (off Low Moor shed, 56F, south of Bradford) climbs up to Copy Pit summit with a Saturdays Only Leeds / Bradford to Blackpool North train on 6 August 1966. This secondary main line between Todmorden and Burnley saw steam workings right through to the end of steam. Note the pristine condition of the locomotive - obviously the work of the "Neverers" of whom the photographer Ken

Another sylvan setting, this time in the south of England just east of Parkstone station. BR Standard Class 5MT 4-6-0 No 73054 has just left Parkstone station and is climbing the steep bank up to Branksome with a local train for Bournemouth off the Somerset & Dorset line. 27 March 1965

(Ken Hale)

On 26 September 1966, ex LMS Class 2MT 2-6-0 No 46442 banks a Halesowen - Stourbridge goods (hauled by ex GWR Class 5700 0-6-0PT No 4696) up the steep bank out of Halesowen, and is just about to enter Hayden Hill tunnel. The other side of the tunnel is where the Halesowen branch joined the old GWR Snow Hill to Stourbridge Junction line at Old Hill station. At Old Hill No 4696 will leave the train, which will then be taken forward to Stourbridge by No 46442. The Halesowen branch closed in 1969. (*Roger Siviter*)

A few days later, on 3 October 1966, and we see Class 5700 0-6-0PT, No 9774. The locomotive has just left Hayden Hill tunnel and is running light engine down to Halesowen, having hauled a Halesowen to Stourbridge goods train up to Old Hill, banked by 2-6-0 No 46470, the 2-6-0 then taking the train forward to Stourbridge. The closure of Tysley shed (2A) to steam in November 1966 saw the end of steam working on the Halesowen branch, and indeed the Birmingham area. *(Roger Siviter)*

Top: On 5 November 1965, ex LNER Class V2 2-6-2 No 60970 climbs the 1 in 80 up to Whitrope summit, just north of Riccarton Junction on the Waverley route, with the 11.15 Carlisle (Kingmoor) to Edinburgh (Millerhill) freight train. Within a few weeks, scenes like this would be history, with steam working on this famous route scheduled to finish by the end of 1965.   *(Ken Hale)*

Bottom: This was the scene at Stranraer shed (67F) on 7 September 1964, with three different Classes of 4-6-0s lined up outside the shed. On the left is BR Standard Class 5MT 4-6-0 No 73077 (behind which are 4-6-0s Nos 45126 and 44999). In the centre is the ex LMS "Black Five" 4-6-0 No 45384, and completing the scene is ex LMS Jubilee Class 4-6-0 No 45742 *Connaught*.   *(Hugh Ballantyne)*

Top: A meeting of ex LNER Gresley Class J38 0-6-0s just outside Thornton Junction on the line to Dunfermline. In the background can be seen Thornton shed (62A) coaling tower. This picture, taken on 21 June 1966, shows on the left No 65929 heading for Thornton with a scrap train from Dunfermline, whilst on the right is No 65914 with a coal train bound for Dunfermline. *(Roger Siviter)*

Bottom: There was still steam traction to be seen in Ayrshire throughout 1966. On 24 June of that year, 4-6-0 No 44989 threads Annbank junction (just east of Ayr) with a mixed freight from Mauchline and Auchinleck. Branching off to the right is the line to Drongan and Killoch. Steam workings in the area finished by the end of 1966 with the closure of Ayr shed (67C). *(Roger Siviter)*

Left: It seems as though winter was late in arriving in 1966, as this picture at Farnley shed (55C) Leeds, taken on 2 April 1966, will bear witness. Jubilee Class 4-6-0 No 45581 *Bihar and Orissa* is seen by the coaling tower on that very wintry day. By this time, most of the surviving Jubilees were shedded in the Leeds area, mainly at Leeds Holbeck shed (55A). The final members of this famous class were withdrawn from service in the autumn of 1967. However, several members remain in preservation.   *(Roger Siviter)*

Above: A cold but bright autumn day at Shrewsbury (25 October 1966) as BR Standard Class 4MT 4-6-0 No 75016 reverses into the station to take out the down "Cambrian Coast Express". No "visi-vest" on the track lookout man, but a white armband. Note the elegant LNWR signal box, Shrewsbury being a joint GWR / LMS station.   *(Roger Siviter)*

Top & Bottom Left: These two pictures show well what the WCML looked like in the Tebay / Dillicar and Low Gill areas, before the advent of the M6 motorway and of course electrification. The first scene, taken on 16 September 1966, shows a north bound van train hauled by ex LMS 5MT 4-6-0 No 45187 as it runs over Dillicar water troughs just south of Tebay. Where the photographer is standing is now part of the M6 motorway.

A couple of miles south of the previous picture is the area known as Low Gill. On 31 August 1967, 4-6-0 No 45353 heads south with an up goods train. This scene, if viewed today, would show that the immediate background is once again the M6 motorway.

(Two pictures: Roger Siviter)

Above: "Black Five" 4-6-0 No 44767 climbs up to Ais Gill summit on 18 July 1967 with a south bound mineral train. The train is just crossing the short Ais Gill viaduct. This locomotive is one of several members of this famous class to be preserved, and can be seen in action on page 95, then numbered 4767 and named *George Stephenson*. *(Ken Hale)*

71/72) Sir William Stanier's Jubilee Class 4-6-0s, introduced on the LMS in 1934, were to be found at work in both the north and the south of the BR network. This first picture shows No 45672 *Anson* passing the fine looking LMS bracket signal at Winwick junction, north of Crewe, with a down unidentified express taking the main line towards Preston on 29 August 1964.

The second scene, taken at Standish junction in Gloucestershire, shows No 45602 *British Honduras* with the 09.00 (Saturdays Only) Paignton to Leeds train. On the left are the GWR lines to Swindon. Note the mixture of stock, including LNER carriages. 9 August 1964.

(*Two pictures: Hugh Ballantyne*)

Top: Ex SR Class U 2-6-0 No 31873 arrives at Dorking Town station with the 15.04 Redhill to Reading train on 22 October 1964. Note the staggered platforms, and also the station lamp and the porter's trolley.

(Hugh Ballantyne)

Bottom: On 10 October 1964, ex GWR Class 5700 0-6-0 No 9711 pauses at Cashes Green Halt with the 13.08 Gloucester Central to Chalford train. This station is a good example of a GWR halt, complete with wooden platforms and corrugated iron platform shelter. At one time, these could be found all over the GWR system.

(Hugh Ballantyne)

Below: Bulleid Merchant Navy Class Class Pacific No 35013 *Blue Funnel* is caught by the camera as it speeds along the former LSWR Bournemouth to Waterloo line near Brockenhurst with an afternoon Waterloo to Weymouth train on Saturday 10 September 1966. I well remember that very sunny late summer day myself, having spent most of it photographing the line around the Pirbright area. A notable visitor to the line that day was LNER Pacific *Flying Scotsman* with the "Farnborough Flyer", a special train from the east Midlands to the Farnborough air show.

(*Ken Hale*)

Above: A fine telephoto shot of Class 8F 2-8-0 No 48425 as it climbs up to Horton - in - Ribblesdale on the S & C route with a mixed north bound goods train. 27 July 1967.

(*Ken Hale*)

Above, Opposite Top Right, Opposite Bottom Right: These next three pictures should, I hope, serve as a reminder of how much trackwork was in place in steam days. The first picture, taken on Sunday 26 June 1966, shows Merchant Navy Pacific No 35026 *Lamport & Holt Line* as it approaches Lapworth station with the final leg of "The Aberdonian" railtour, terminating at Waterloo. This special train was organised by the Warwickshire Railway Society, and started from Waterloo at 22.30 on Friday 24 June and ran as far north as Aberdeen, covering many routes and using a wide variety of steam locomotives. This ex GWR four track section from Tyseley to Lapworth lasted until 1970, when two of the tracks were taken out.

The next scene was taken at the western end of Skipton station on the 11 July 1966, and shows "Black Five" 4-6-0 No 44912 surrounded by a mass of trackwork and various infrastructure, etc.

The final picture, taken on 17 July 1966, shows 4-6-0 No 45255 on station pilot duties at Manchester Victoria station. These duties were mainly banking heavy trains up Miles Platting bank on the line to Stalybridge and Leeds. As with most large stations in those late steam days, there was still a large amount of trackwork. This station has now been virtually rebuilt, and this scene is unrecognisable today.

(Three pictures: Roger Siviter)

Above & Right: Sunday 5 March 1967 saw the end of the through workings between Paddington and Chester / Birkenhead via Birmingham Snow Hill and Shrewsbury. To mark the occasion, the Stephenson Locomotive Society (SLS) ran two special trains from Birmingham to Birkenhead and return that day.

The first of the special trains is seen near Codsall (north of Wolverhampton) on the outward journey to Birkenhead. In charge is ex GWR Castle Class 4-6-0 No 7029 *Clun Castle*.

The second special, hauled by ex LMS Class 5MT No 44680, is seen on its return journey as it climbs the 1 in 82 of Gresford bank, just north of Wrexham.   *(Above: Roger Siviter. Right: Ken Hale)*

Ex LMS Class 5MT 4-6-0 No 45135 runs south through the picturesque Lune Valley near Dillicar with an up afternoon mixed freight train on a beautiful September day in 1966 (the 16th). It will be noted that the locomotive is in fine external condition. I had been reliably informed that this was because No 45135 had been on a Royal Train standby duty the previous day.

(Roger Siviter)

On 25 February 1967, Jubilee Class 4-6-0 No 45562 *Alberta* climbs out of Huddersfield and heads for the WCML via Manchester with a Leeds to Carlisle special train - "The Border Countryman". The return to Leeds was via the S & C route. This train was organised by the Jubilee Locomotive Preservation Society.

(Ken Hale)

Top: "Black Five" 4-6-0 No 44872 hurries along near Charwelton (Northants) with the 08.15 Nottingham Victoria to London Marylebone train on the last day of the through services on the Great Central route. Saturday 3 September 1966. *(Roger Siviter)*

Bottom: A rather woebegone looking BR Standard Class 4MT 2-6-0 No 76039 heads west with the down Cambrian Coast Express on 2 July 1966. The location is Trewern near Breiddan, just to the east of Welshpool.

(Roger Siviter)

Top: Another workstained locomotive, this time ex LNER Class V2 2-6-2 No 60824, seen south of Shankend on the Waverley route with the 08.16 Edinburgh Millerhill to Carlisle Kingmoor freight train on 23 October 1965.　(*Ken Hale*)

Bottom: Class 8F WD 2-8-0 No 90625 approaches Wakefield Kirkgate on 22 September 1966 with coal from the Goole area. On the left hand side is the line to Normanton.

(*Roger Siviter*)

Above & Right: Grayrigg bank between Oxenholme and Grayrigg summit (around seven miles of 1 in 104 to 1 in 120) would see the use of banking locomotives on heavy goods trains until the end of steam in the area, on 31 December 1967.

The first picture, taken on a very dull 14 September 1966, shows 4-6-0 No 44948 as it climbs out of Oxenholme with a morning down goods train. The location is where the A684 to Hawes crosses over the line.

Banking assistance is provided by an ex LMS Fairburn Class 4MT 2-6-4T.

Two days later, on 16 September 1966, and we have sunny weather as Class 4MT 2-6-4T No 42251 banks a heavy ballast train up Grayrigg bank. The train locomotive is Class 8F 2-8-0 No 48731.

(Two pictures: Roger Siviter)

Left: This final selection of pictures were all taken in 1968 - the final months of BR steam, which was centred around the north west of England. This was the scene at the southern end of Preston station on the morning of 26 February 1968 with "Black Five" 4-6-0 No 44890 waiting to take out the 12.17 Preston to Manchester and Liverpool. This train which originated in Glasgow was one of the last rostered steam passenger workings. *(Roger Siviter)*

Above: On a misty Saturday 9 March 1968, ex LMS Class 8F 2-8-0 No 48652, complete with snow plough, runs light engine through Manchester Victoria station.

(Roger Siviter)

Left: BR Standard Class 9F 2-10-0 No 92167 peers out of Carnforth shed (10A) on the morning of 16 April 1968. There were still some steam freight workings on the Furness line until the end of BR steam. *(Roger Siviter)*

Top Right: A smart looking BR Standard Class 4MT 4-6-0 No 75019 runs through Clapham (Yorks) with a train of empty ore wagons bound for Skipton and Swinden Quarry on the Grassington branch. Nos 75019 and 75027 were both shedded at Carnforth in order to work these ore trains to and from Swinden Quarry and were kept in fine external condition by enthusiasts. 17 April 1968.

(Roger Siviter)

Bottom Right: A route that saw steam activity right through to the end was the Preston / Blackburn / Burnley line. On 6 June 1968, Class 8F 2-8-0 No 48294 climbs the 1 in 101 near Hoghton and heads for Burnley with a train of coal empties from the Preston area.

(Roger Siviter)

Left: "Black Five" 4-6-0 No 44890 is busy shunting vans at Manchester Victoria station on 9 March 1968. These Class 5MT 4-6-0s were designed by Sir William Stanier and introduced on the LMS in 1934. As can be seen in the pictures at Rainhill (pages 2 and 88) they lasted until the very end of BR steam. Several examples of this "maid of all work" locomotive have survived in preservation. *(Roger Siviter)*

Above: Next to Victoria station was Manchester Exchange station (they were connected by the longest platform in the UK). BR Standard Class 5MT 4-6-0 No 73157 (fitted with Caprotti valve gear) pauses during shunting duties at Exchange station on 9 March 1968. This locomotive was shedded at Manchester Patricroft (9H) which closed at the end of June 1968. *(Roger Siviter)*

Top Left, Bottom Left & Above: A visit to Skelton junction (near Stockport) on the former Cheshire Lines Committee (CLC) route on 25 April 1968 saw a fair amount of activity with Class 8Fs on mainly coal trains, etc. This first picture shows No 48322 near Skelton junction with a west bound coal train.

Earlier on that day, and we see No 48115 with a west bound mixed goods train near Baguley, east of Skelton junction.

The final picture is a side view of No 48723 as it hurries towards Skelton junction with a west bound coal train. Steam workings finished in this area around the early part of June 1968. These ex LMS Stanier designed 2-8-0 freight locomotives were first introduced in 1935 and survived until the end of BR steam. Several examples of the class have been preserved.

(Three pictures: Roger Siviter)

Left: One of the last locomotive sheds to close was Lostock Hall (10D) at Preston. On the evening of 19 July 1968, 4-6-0 No 44806 runs past the coaling tower as it leaves the shed.

(*Roger Siviter*)

Above: Earlier that year, on Sunday 25 February 1968, one of Lostock Hall's allocation of "Black Fives" No 45345 waits to leave Preston station with the 17.52 to Liverpool.

(*Roger Siviter*)

Above: Almost the end at Rose Grove shed (10F) as 8F 2-8-0s Nos 48723 and 48167 wait in the shed yard for possible work on 19 July 1968.   (*Roger Siviter*)

Top Right: On Saturday 4 August 1968, a series of special trains were run by various railway societies to mark the end of steam. The SLS ran two specials, the first of which, headed by 4-6-0s Nos 44874 and 45017, is seen near Saddleworth heading for Huddersfield.   (*Ken Hale*)

Bottom Right: For three years after the end of steam, the only steam locomotive to run on BR was LNER Pacific No 4472 *Flying Scotsman*. One of the first trips it made within a few weeks of the end of steam was on 29 September 1968, and that was a Tyseley to Leamington Spa train (run in connection with Tyseley Open Day), seen here on the outward journey on the four track section near Lapworth.   (*Roger Siviter*)

Thousands of people turned out to see the very last BR steam train on 11 August 1968. The "15 Guinea Special" is seen here arriving at the historic station of Rainhill (site of the 1830 locomotive trials) with an ex LMS "Black Five" No 45110 in charge for the Liverpool to Manchester section of this notable train. (See also picture on page 2). Britannia Pacific No 70013 *Oliver Cromwell* would be in charge from Manchester to Carlisle (via the S & C) and the return journey would be in the hands of 4-6-0s Nos 44871 and 44781.

(*Roger Siviter*)

Top: Ex SR West Country Pacific No 34013 *Oakhampton* looks a treat as it stands at Westbury waiting to work an LCGB special train from Waterloo to Maiden Newton, part of the "Bridport Belle" tour of 22 January 1967, Maiden Newton being the junction for the Bridport branch, where a pair of Ivatt Class 2-6-2Ts took over for the journey on the branch line. *(Hugh Ballantyne)*

Bottom: Southern Region steam finished on 9 July 1967. To mark the occasion, SR ran two "Farewell to Steam" special trains from Waterloo to Bournemouth and return on Sunday 2 July 1967. The second of these two special workings is seen on its return working (16.30 ex Bournemouth) passing Pokesdown, just east of Bournemouth. In charge is Merchant Navy Pacific No 35028 *Clan Line*, now happily preserved. *(Hugh Ballantyne)*

Above: On 28 March 1968, "Black Five" 4-6-0 No 44781 passes Skew Bridge signal box near Preston with the Glasgow to Manchester train, steam hauled from Preston. *(Hugh Ballantyne)*

Below: Ex LMS Class 8F 2-8-0 No 48253 hauling a breakdown train heads south past Lostock Hall Station signal box. 28 March 1968. *(Hugh Ballantyne)*

Top: For the three year period between August 1968 and October 1971 when, with the exception of *Flying Scotsman* (see picture on page 87) steam was not allowed to run on the main line, the nearest we got to it was theTyseley Museum Open Day, when a steam shuttle service ran from the shed area to the junction for the North Warwicks line.

On Sunday 17 May 1970, LMS Jubilee Class 4-6-0 No 5593 *Kholapur* heads past Tyseley station with the shuttle service assisted in the rear by LMS Class 5MT 4-6-0 No 5420, then named after the doyen of railway photographers, *Eric Treacy*. (*Roger Siviter*)

Right: Steamtown Carnforth (the old steam shed10A) plays host to LNER Class A3 Pacific *Flying Scotsman* on 11 July 1978. No 4472 would shortly be working the outward leg of the "Cambrian Coast Express" from Carnforth to Ravenglass. (*Roger Siviter*)

Top: Unlike some areas, steam only returned to Devon and Cornwall in 1985 and now, although Devon sees a fair amount of special trains, steam specials in Cornwall are a much rarer occurrence. However, on 7 April 2007, we see GWR King Class 4-6-0 No 6024 *King Edward I* and GWR Castle Class 4-6-0 No 5051 *Earl Bathurst* as they head away from Lyhner viaduct near Saltash with a Penzance to Bristol train. This was the first leg of the "Great Britain" tour, with a wide variety of steam haulage from Penzance to Wick and Thurso. In the background is the River Lyhner. *(Roger Siviter)*

Bottom On 3 July 1983, GWR Castle Class 4-6-0 No 5051, then named *Drysllwyn Castle*, runs through Marshbrook with a Newport to Shrewsbury special, "The Welsh Dragon". *(Christina Siviter)*

Top: BR Standard Britannia Class Pacific No 70000 *Britannia* is photographed just south of Hellifield as it heads towards Blackburn with an Appleby to Lostock (Preston) special charter train, "The Cumbrian Mountain Express". 7 September 1991.
(Roger Siviter)

Bottom: The unique BR Standard Class 8P Pacific No 71000 *Duke of Gloucester* passes by Conway Castle with the east bound "North Wales Coast Express" from Holyhead to Crewe on 25 July 1990.
(Roger Siviter)

Top: Beautifully restored former S & D Class 7F 2-8-0 No 13809 climbs out of Carnforth East junction on 30 April 1983, and heads for Hellifield with the lower leg of the north bound "Cambrian Mountain Pullman" train, the north bound section from Hellifield to Carlisle being hauled by ex SR West Country Pacific No 34092 *City of Wells*.

(*Christina Siviter*)

Bottom: The south bound "Aberdonian" from Perth to Edinburgh accelerates through Stirling station with ex LNER Class A2 4-6-2 'No 60532 *Blue Peter* in charge. Note the fine selection of semaphore signals. 17 October 1993.

(*Roger Siviter*)

Top: On the evening of 6 June 1981, "Black Five" 4-6-0 No 4767 *George Stephenson* crosses the High Level Bridge at Newcastle with a train for Hexham and return. This was the fourth and final working of the day to celebrate the 200th anniversary of the birth of George Stephenson on 9 June 1781. (*Christina Siviter*)

Bottom: Journey's end for the Toyota train from Inverness to Kyle of Lochalsh, hauled by "Black Five" No 5025 on 5 October 1982. Dominating the background is the Isle of Skye.

(*Roger Siviter*)

Top: SR King Arthur Class 4-6-0 No 777 *Sir Lamiel* works hard on its old stamping ground, the former LSWR line from Waterloo to Exeter. The location is North Perrott, to the east of Crewekerne, and the train is an Andover to Exeter special charter. 28 June 1992.   *(Roger Siviter)*

Bottom: The final picture was taken at Tavistock junction Plymouth, on the evening of 24 August 2007. The train is a return Par to Bristol charter "The Eden Limited" hauled by ex SR West Country Class 4-6-2 No 34067 *Tangmere* and GWR King Class 4-6-0 No 6024 *King Edward I.*   *(Roger Siviter)*